STAY TRUE

An interactive children's guide to staying true to yourself

Written by Salpi Dunlap

Illustrated by London Dunlap

Copyright Text © 2018 Salpi Dunlap

Copyright Illustrations © 2018 London Dunlap

Edited by Michael Molenda

Third edition printed in 2022

All rights reserved. No part of this publication may be reproduced or transmitted in any form or by any means, mechanical or electronic, including photocopying, recording, or otherwise, or stored in a retrieval system, without prior permission from the publisher.

For more information, contact:
Salpi Dunlap
salpi@staytruebooks.com
www.staytruebooks.com

ISBN: 978-0-578-40730-2

INSPIRATION

We have this conversation every morning before I drop my three kids off at school. I ask what "staying true" means to them. They always answer with the messages on the following pages of this book. I like reminding them of how special and unique they are, and how they hold an exceptional place in this world.

STAY TRUE

FOREWORD

This book is meant to be read *with* your child. It's also meant to span all ages. Your child may need a little explanation here and there. Feel free to fill in the blanks for them. The questions in each section are meant to promote conversation and connection with your child. Every time you read the book together, something new will be learned!

This book can be read every night with different outcomes and points of discussion. Use the questions on each page to stay present, learn about each other's day, and practice gratitude. Repetitive reading will reinforce the lessons set forth in this book. Focus on your child's day. Evoke healthy communication. Build confidence and self-esteem.

It's so important to empower kids to take control of their emotions. In a current world surrounded by so much stress, competition, and anxiety, kids can learn to quiet their minds with deep breathing and turning their thoughts inward.

Your child may want to read this book alone (especially the older ones). Let them! Let them find their own inspiration. You can always ask them about their experience with it for a chance to keep the connection as they get older.

Kids love to be heard! Let them talk. Just listen. You'll be surprised at what comes out. Recognizing and appreciating their good qualities are important first steps toward building confidence and self-esteem. Choosing love over fear in any situation will help kids practice gratitude and own their feelings.

What is intrinsic motivation? Intrinsic motivation is behavior that is driven by internal rewards. Use positive reinforcement, provide honest and instructive feedback on their projects, help them set goals, and encourage collaboration with friends and family members. These steps will empower your child with the feeling of conscious choice.

STAY TRUE

ACKNOWLEDGEMENTS

First and foremost, I would like to thank my children. Without them, I wouldn't be the person I've become today. I will be forever grateful for them. Thank you to my daughter, London, who at ten years old created the beautiful images in this book. Thank you to my boys, Logan and Lincoln, for helping me review and edit the content. Thanks to my truest friend, Vania Frank, for her love and faith in me, and to my mentor, Victor Oddo, for his guidance and enthusiasm for this project. And thank you, my dear readers, for your support!

DEDICATION

This book is dedicated to everyone who has ever had the privilege of influencing a child.

STAY TRUE

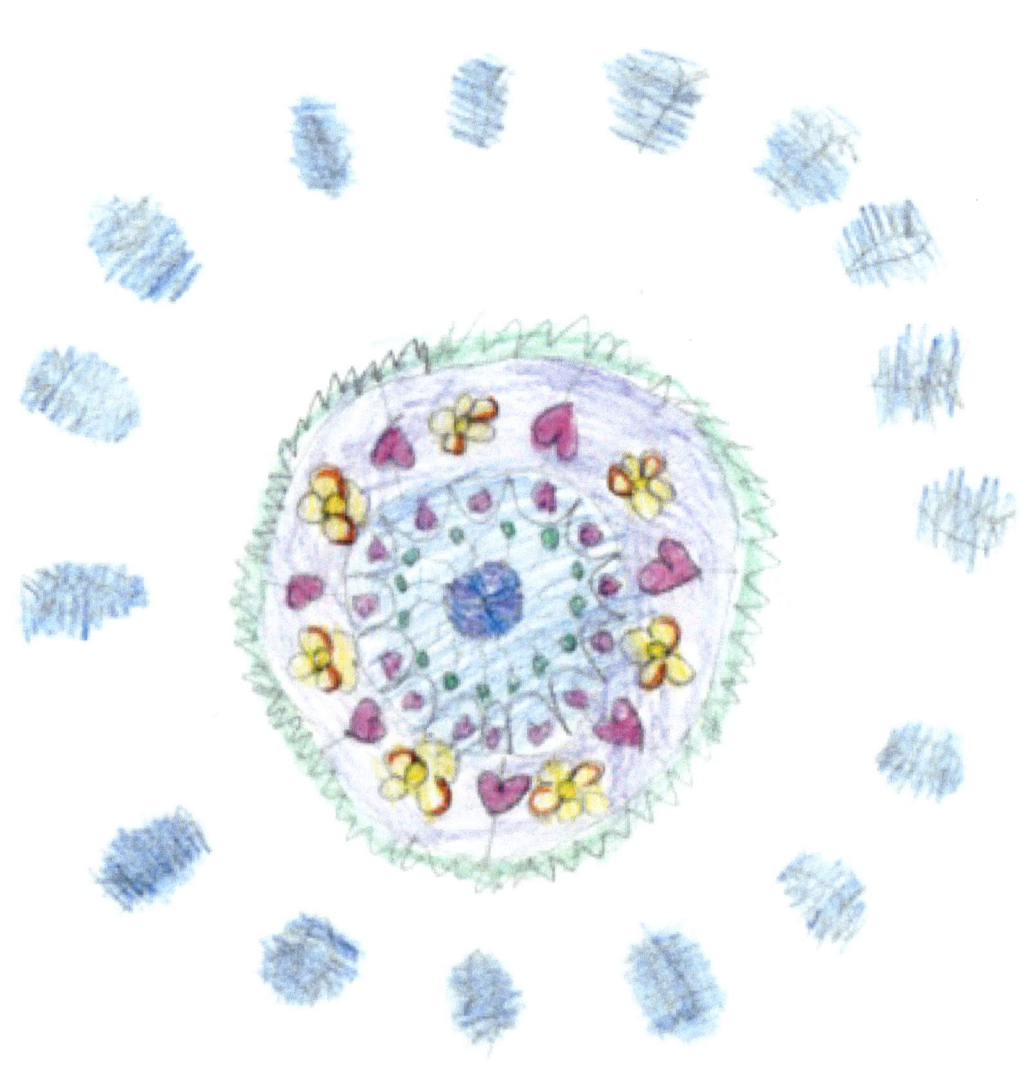

x

BREATHE

A good way to start just about *anything* is to take a minute to focus on your breathing. Try it now. Take a deep breath in through your nose. Breathe out slowly through your mouth while relaxing your body. Really feel your body relax.

This is something you can practice every day and every night. It's a good way to relax, focus, and stay true. Do it a few times before you start turning the pages of this book.

STAY TRUE

BE YOURSELF

There are almost eight billion people on this planet, and only *one* you. You are unique. You are special. Take some time to think about how you are different than your friends and siblings. What are some of your unique qualities and strengths? These qualities can change and grow everyday as you learn new things!

Focus on your strengths, but also remember that no one is perfect. Everyone has faults, and the mistakes we make help us learn and grow. The universe wants *you* to shine. So let yourself shine! Don't compare yourself with other people. It doesn't matter what others think. Just be YOU!

STAY TRUE

BE KIND

When things don't go your way, don't be too hard on yourself. Know that everything will work out the way it should. You can choose to see a situation through love, rather than fear. Turn a negative mindset into a positive mindset. Be kind to yourself.

Be kind to others, as well. Show kindness to everyone around you. Animals, too! Pick up litter. Smile at friends. Say "please" and "thank you." Support others in school, at work, and at home. Take care of your bedroom, your home, your family, your pets, and your friends.

STAY TRUE

BELIEVE IN YOURSELF

Love yourself. Unconditionally. Practice saying, "I love myself," right now. Say it until you feel it and believe it. Loving yourself goes hand in hand with *believing* in yourself. When you are having a hard time with something, remind yourself that everything will be okay. Let the past go and keep moving forward.

Remember, there's an inner voice inside you that believes in you, too. When your mind is quiet, you can hear it. This is best done with meditation. Meditation is just a fancy word for closing your eyes, focusing on your breathing, relaxing your body, and quieting your mind. Anyone can do it! You can start by practicing for one minute at a time. This way, your brain will relax, and you'll be able to hear what your inner voice is trying to tell you.

FOLLOW YOUR HEART

Do things that make you happy. Chase butterflies. Climb rainbows. Catch stars. Find time every day to do things you enjoy. Have you followed your heart today?

A good way to follow your heart is by working on your passion— something that brings you joy. What do you love to do? What is one thing you would do every day if you could?

Take some time every day to work on your passion. You may even have more than one passion! You can work on as many as you want. Don't let fear stop you from doing the things that bring you joy.

STAY TRUE

SHOW YOUR EMOTIONS

We have a lot of different emotions inside of us, and they can come out at any time. It's okay to show all of your different emotions. When you are happy and excited, let it show! Enjoy these moments! It's okay to feel mad or sad, too. But always remember to be honest about your feelings.

You see, you have the power to control your actions and reactions. You have no control over other people's actions and reactions, but you always have the choice to control your own. If someone upsets you, of course, you will be upset. But you can choose not to *stay* upset. Focus on something that makes you happy and move on. Life will not always be easy, but you will get through it. It helps to talk about your feelings and emotions with someone you trust. Never be afraid to ask for help!

TRY YOUR BEST

I'm sure you've heard the phrases "try your best" and "give it your all." But what do they mean? They can mean you should do everything you can to make something work. Or they can encourage you to work hard and don't give up.

But, even if you fail, keep trying! Wayne Gretzky, the famous hockey player, once said, "You miss 100 percent of the shots you don't take." So, keep trying!

Always tell yourself that you will do your best. That's all you can do. Then, go out there and give it your best! If you think of failing as a learning tool, you will find success eventually.

STAY TRUE

BE PRESENT

Being present means living in the moment. Focus on your surroundings, your actions, and your thoughts in the present time—*not* in the past or future.

Learn from your past experiences and then let them go. Thinking too much about the future can turn into worrying and worrying about something will not change it.

As long as you make the right choices—if you are kind, if you try your best, and if you follow your gut—the universe will rise up to meet you. Trust yourself.

REMEMBER YOUR INNER CHILD

Play! Laugh! Be silly! Use your imagination and get creative!

Don't ever lose that wonder you have. Never stop exploring and asking questions. Continue to learn new things and have new experiences. This goes for adults, too! Remind the adults in your life to play and do things that bring them joy every day.

How did you play today? Were you inside or outside? Who did you play with? How did you use your imagination? What did you create today?

DO THE RIGHT THING

Deep inside you, there's a little voice that knows what's right and what's wrong. Do you listen to that voice? Sometimes, doing the right thing is difficult, but you always have the choice to do good.

Can you think of any examples where you made a right choice? How about a wrong choice? If you make a wrong choice, how do you fix it? Most of the time, an apology works best.

TAKE RESPONSIBILITY

Own your actions! When you make a decision, think about how that decision will affect you, as well as others.

An easy way to take responsibility is to do the right thing. If you make a bad choice, remember there are ways to fix it—such as admitting your bad choice and apologizing for it.

STAY TRUE

BE GRATEFUL

Being grateful means focusing on the positive things in your life. Practicing gratefulness everyday will help you stay true and happy. What are you thankful for in this moment? What was your favorite part of the day? How could you have made your day *even better?*

Create a Gratitude Journal by decorating a notebook and writing in it every day. Start by writing three things you're grateful for each day.

MISTAKES, SCHMISTAKES!

True story. London (our illustrator) was busy drawing one of the pages for this book when she made a mistake. She had put so much effort into getting this far, and she had already made so much progress that she didn't want to start over.

What did she do in that "mistake moment"?

Well, she got a bit upset, a bit sad, and almost felt like giving up. But instead of letting those feelings take over, she paused for a minute, took a deep breath, and looked over her work. By doing this, she was able to change a negative mindset to a positive mindset. She changed the way she thought about her mistake, and found a clever way to fix it. I bet you can't even find it!

STAY TRUE

STAND STRONG

"Stand Strong" encompasses all the other phrases in this book and it completes the big picture. Love yourself, believe in yourself, try your best, be kind, and believe that great things are on their way. Stand strong in your actions, your feelings, and your beliefs. You are an amazing person. No one can take that away from you. So, do YOU!

STAY TRUE

MANTRAS

A mantra is a word or sound that is repeated during meditation. We can use mantras to help us build confidence and self-esteem. Practice saying the following mantras to yourself every morning and every night. Practice with your adults, too! Say them in front of a mirror! Focus on how you feel when you say these words...

I am loved.
I am beautiful.
I love myself.
I matter.
I am important.
I am unique.
I am special.

STAY TRUE

ABOUT THE AUTHOR

Salpi is the mother of three beautiful children. She started on her spiritual journey years ago, but didn't realize it until 2016. Since then, she has started practicing being grateful and present. Gratitude and living in the moment have really changed her perspective on happiness. Her quality of life has greatly improved, and all she really did was change the way she looks at things.

Her intent is to share this message with people of all ages. It's never too early or too late to start staying true.

Her daughter and middle child, London, is the illustrator of their book. Salpi wrote the words, and then asked her daughter to draw whatever came to mind to portray the words on the page. The result was pure magic.

www.ingramcontent.com/pod-product-compliance
Lightning Source LLC
Chambersburg PA
CBHW061403090426
42743CB00003B/128